SCRATCHES

My New Life!

By:

Dede Stockton
and
LaRae Musselman

Illustrated by Gaspar Sabater

Copyright © 2019 by Dede Stockton/DreamMaker Books LLC

All rights reserved. No part of this publication may be reproduced, distributed or transmitted in any form or by any means, including photocopying, recording, or other electronic or mechanical methods, without the prior written per-mission of the publisher, except in the case of brief quotations embodied in critical reviews and certain other noncommercial uses permitted by copyright law. For permission requests, write to the publisher, addressed "Attention: Permissions Coordinator," at the address below.

Dede Stockton, LaRae Musselman
DreamMaker Books LLC
5563 S. Uravan Ct.
Centennial, CO 80015

www.dreammakerbook.com
www.sammijoadventures.com
www.dedestockton.com

Cover Design and Illustrations - Gaspar Sabater gasparsabater@gmail.com

Ordering Information: Special discounts are available on quantity purchases by corporations, associations, and others. For details, contact the publisher at the address above.

Quantity sales. Special discounts are available on quantity purchases by corporations, associations, schools and others. For details, contact Dede Stockton at the address listed above.

Scratches- My New Life/ Dede Stockton and LaRae Musselman — 1st edition

ISBN: 978-0-9995834-4-9 (paperback)
ISBN: 978-0-9995834-5-6 (hardback)
ISBN: 978-0-9995834-6-3 (EBook)

Scratches had the best life a horse could ask for!

He lived on a ranch high in the beautiful mountains of Colorado.

He had a whole field full of mares and foals he got to watch after.

He had a best friend that came to visit and ride him every day.

And ...

He got to help his rancher round up cattle at least a couple of times a week.

He glanced around his fields and gave a deep snort of satisfaction.

Scratches LOVED his life on the ranch!

WHOA!! What is that? He thought to himself.

Silently creeping through the grass was a large mountain lion!

Scratches had saved his mares and the beautiful little foal that was hiding behind his mom!

The bad news is that Scratches had cut his foot badly while he was rearing and stomping to scare away the lion.

He stood there panting and heaving as he lifted his badly injured foot.

It hurt so bad he wasn't sure he was going to be able to walk.

Grandma arrived within a few minutes and the rancher and the vet showed up right behind her.

After a lot of talking and head scratching, they finally decided to bandage his hurt foot and try to find him a home with people who could love and care for him while he healed.

Scratches could feel that his life was about to change, and he was beginning to feel a little scared ...

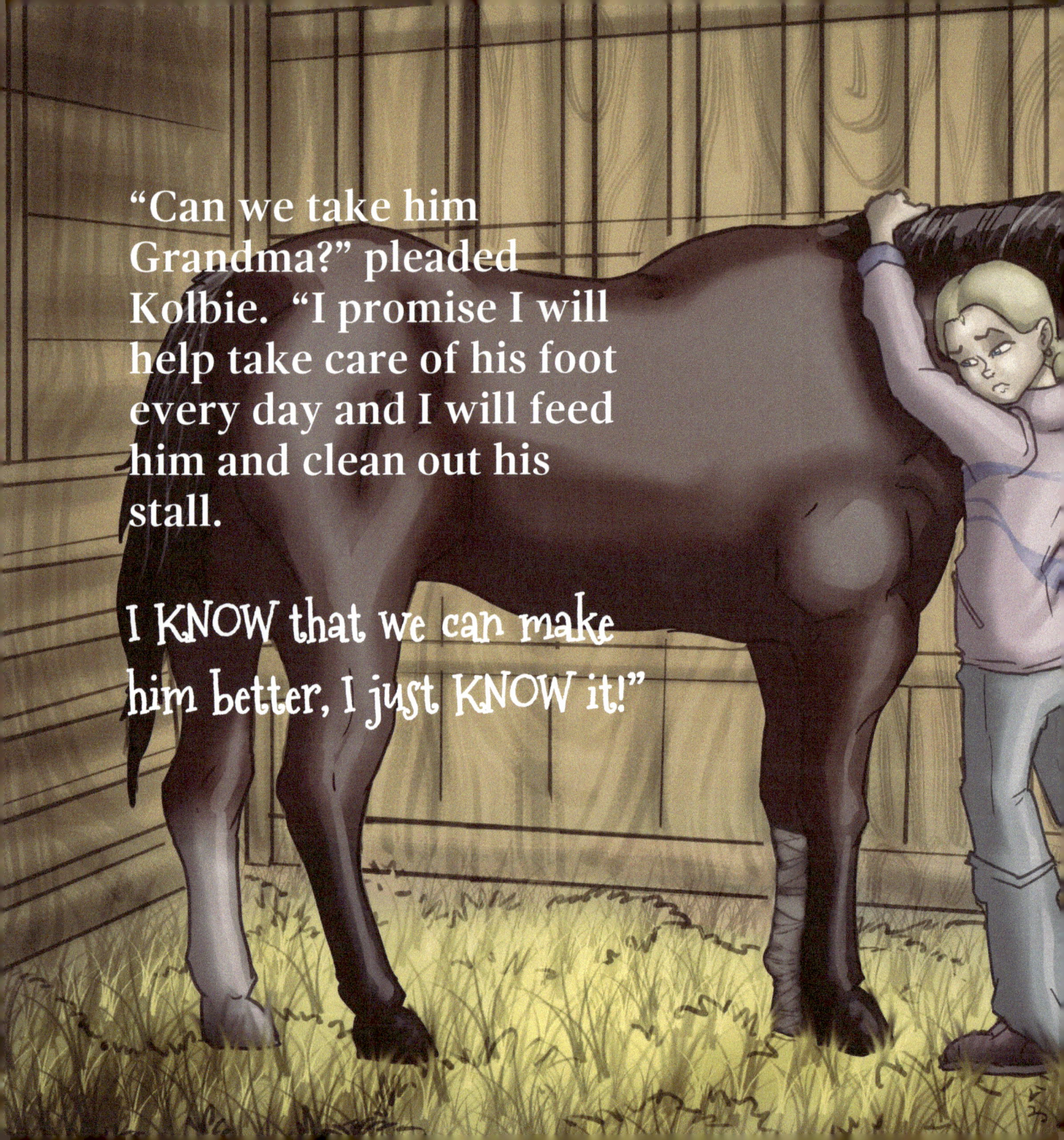

Scratches seemed a little confused about his new home but was eating well and his foot was getting better every day!

Kolbie and Grandma were super excited!

But ...

They did!!

Scratches seemed very surprised the day they put a little goat in his corral. And ... was *shocked* when she immediately jumped into his hay trough.

Every day Grandma would take Scratches for a walk so that he could begin using his foot more and Daisy would cry because she didn't get to go.

Scratches soon refused to go without her, so with Kolbie's help, they began taking Daisy along for the walks!

Both Scratches and Daisy enjoyed this time together a lot!

And then, one dark night, something scary happened!

Scratches woke up to find that Daisy was gone! He searched EVERYWHERE but couldn't find her!

He whinnied as loud as he could, but no one from the house came – so he knocked down one of the fence sections and went searching for her himself!

It wasn't long before he found poor little Daisy crying in fear at the bottom of a deep hole.

What should Scratches do now?

He nickered at her softly, promising her he would be right back and then turned to trot quickly back to the house.

Scratches stood outside the house whinnying, and soon both Grandma and Kolbie appeared at the door with bright flashlights.

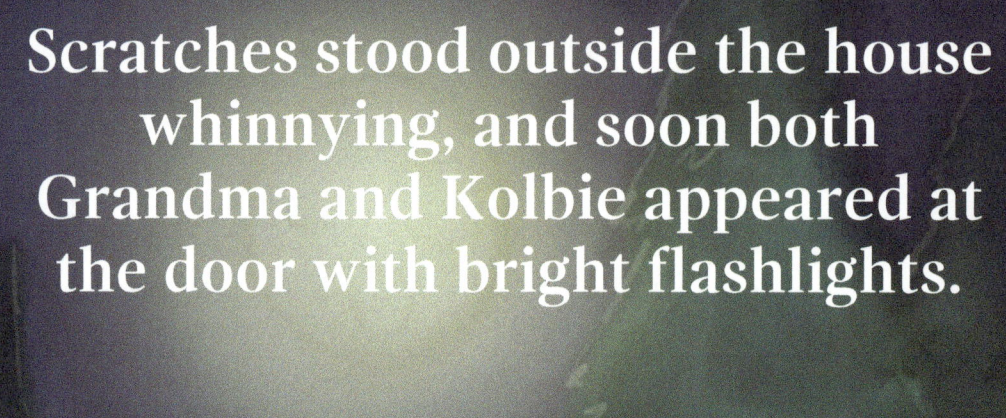

"What's wrong boy?" asked Kolbie, looking around fearfully.

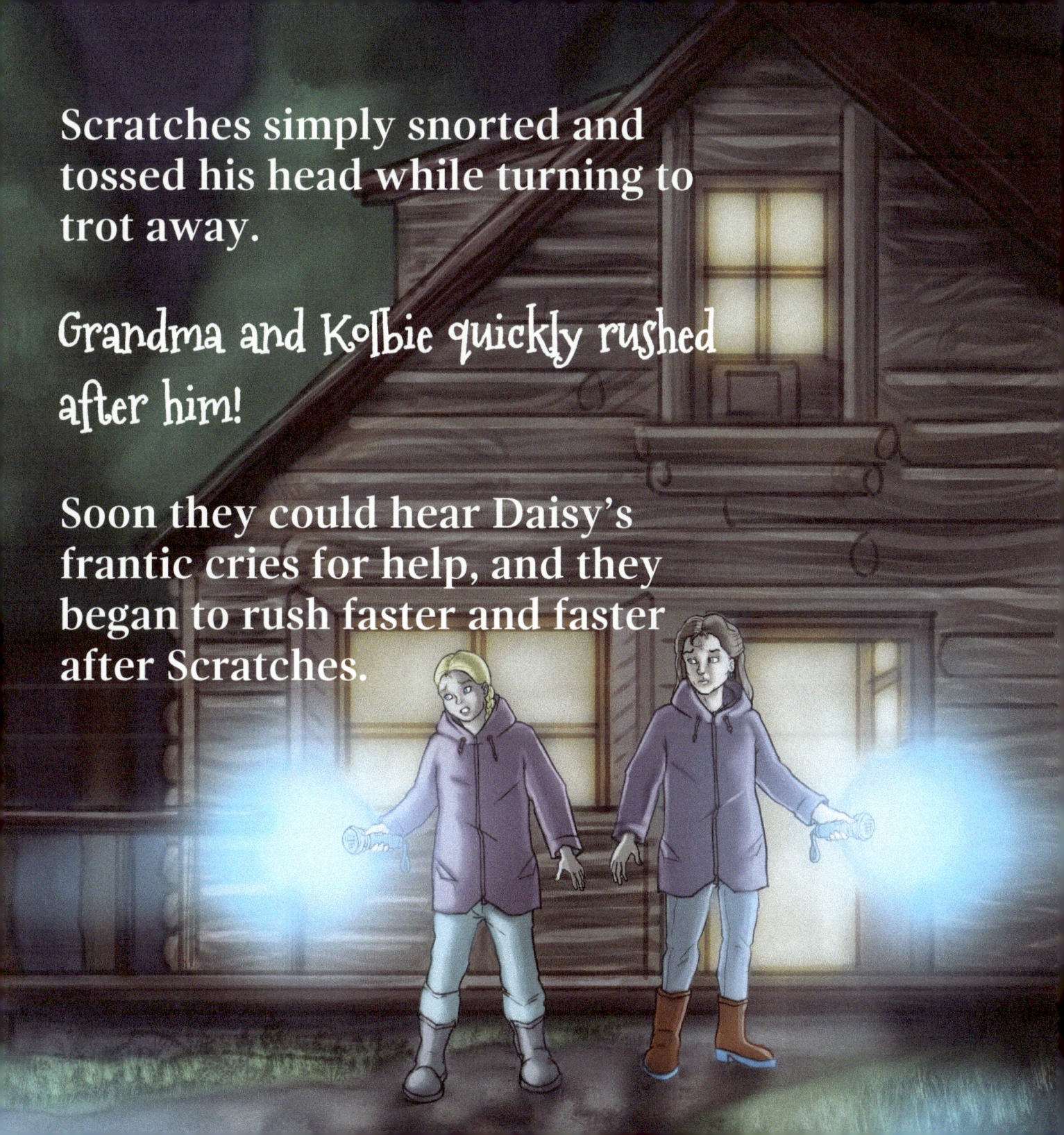

Scratches simply snorted and tossed his head while turning to trot away.

Grandma and Kolbie quickly rushed after him!

Soon they could hear Daisy's frantic cries for help, and they began to rush faster and faster after Scratches.

When they finally reached the hole and looked down at Daisy, they both breathed a sigh of relief. She seemed very scared but did not seem to be hurt!

How would they get her out of the hole!?

As soon as she returned, they put a ladder into the hole and Grandma climbed down.

After giving Daisy lots of hugs, she made a sling out of rope and strips of canvas, wrapped it carefully around her and then rushed back up the ladder.

They tied the other end of the rope around Scratches' neck and Kolbie coaxed Scratches to walk slowly away from the hole.

Soon Daisy was swinging over the top in Grandma's arms!!

Scratches, Daisy, Kolbie and Grandma walked and played in the deep snow drifts around the house.

As fast as Scratches was healing, they might even be able to ride him by next summer!

Who are Scratches, Daisy and Kolbie?

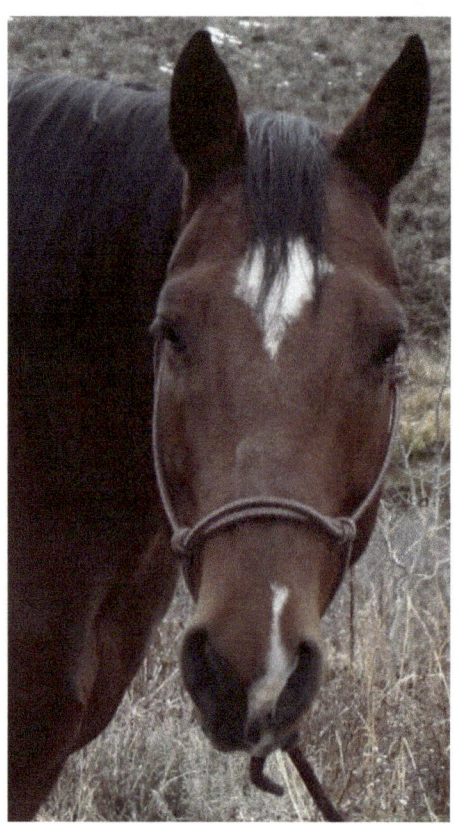

Scratches and Daisy are a real horse and a real goat that live in the mountains of Colorado. The stories of Scratches and Daisy are _loosely based_ upon real life events. Grandma and Kolbie are the people who love and take care of them.

About the Authors

Dede Stockton has written a series of award-winning children's book about a little girl and her friend the sea monster. Look up the *Sammi Jo Adventure Series* on Amazon to learn more.

Dede has been able to follow the journey of Scratches through her good friend, LaRae, and felt that their story would make an amazing picture book!

www.dreammakerbook.com

LaRae Musselman is Grandma and gets to play with and take care of Scratches and Daisy every day! She has given them both a beautiful home and gave Scratches a second chance at life.

LaRae believes firmly in healing through natural methods and works closely with her daughter to help people improve their quality of life!

www.simplyhealthwellness.com

About the Illustrator

Gaspar Sabater is a cartoonist and illustrator, having illustrated numerous children's books, including all the books in the *Sammi Jo Adventure Series*. He lives in Argentina.

Here is the link to his portfolio – just in case you, too, need an awesome illustrator: www.deviantart.com/gasparsabater

CPSIA information can be obtained
at www.ICGtesting.com
Printed in the USA
JSHW011435091119
2312JS00002B/18